Praise for <u>Sonnets from the Dark Lady and Other Poems</u>

"I love these sculpted and energetic poems, full of drama and wit. Many of them are about the author's native New Orleans, which comes alive in them even for someone who, like myself, has never visited that storied city; others are set in the world common to us all, of love, heartbreak, and family. What they all have --- to borrow a phrase from one of them --- is 'that excess, that overflow / inherent in the bearing born of being.'"

−Michael Potemra

Literary Editor, *National Review*

"Having just finished Jennifer Reeser's third book, *Sonnets from the Dark Lady*, I'll just quote the Bard himself in his 20th Sonnet: She is 'the master mistress of my passion.' I think Shakespeare has summed up better than I could my feelings about this book. Buy it and better yet, memorize it."

−Timothy Murphy

Yale Scholar of the House in Poetry

author of <u>Mortal Stakes / Faint Thunder</u>

"Once again, Jennifer Reeser has graced us with a stunning collection of top-notch poetry in a remarkable assortment of styles, forms, and meters. Reeser's villanelles, couplets, quatrains, Sapphic stanzas, heptameters, dactyls, translations—and most prominently, her *tour de force* sonnet sequence in the voice of Shakespeare's Dark Lady—dazzle the reader with poetic rigor and luminous perception. In addition, their wide-ranging allusiveness brings back depth, maturity, and intelligence to a poetry world sorely in need of those things. Reeser is one of the most powerful and compelling voices in genuine poetry today."

− Joseph S. Salemi

Editor, *TRINACRIA*

Sonnets from the Dark Lady and Other Poems

Jennifer Reeser

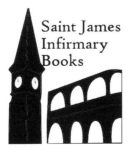

Saint James
Infirmary
Books

Foreword copyright ©2012 by Paul Stevens
Cover Art: *Dark Lady Study in Charcoal* by Jennifer Reeser
Dark Lady Logo & Back Cover Art, *Tudor Rose*, by Kathryn Reeser

First Edition, Feb 2012

Sonnets from the Dark Lady and Other Poems

Copyright ©2012 by Jennifer Reeser

ISBN:978-0615589503

Saint James Infirmary Books
Westlake, Louisiana
editor@saintjamesinfirmary.com

Editor, Mentor, Friend
In Memoriam William F. Carlson

"...even the darkness will not be dark to you; the night will shine
like the day,

for darkness is as light to you. "
Psalm 139:12

Grateful acknowledgment is made to the editors of the journals in which these
poems previously appeared:

*Able Muse, American Arts Quarterly, The Avatar Review, Botteghe Oscure
(Online), Bumbershoot, The Chimaera, Chronicles: A Magazine of American
Culture, Danse Macabre, The Dark Horse, First Things, The Flea, Iambs &
Trochees, LIGHT Quarterly, Lucid Rhythms, The Lyric, Measure, Mezzo
Cammin, The National Review, The Nepotist, POETRY, The Raintown Review,
SCR, THINK Journal, TRINACRIA, Tucumcari Literary Review, Umbrella,
Unsplendid*

Table of Contents

Let me declare two strong biases: firstly, for me, Shakespeare's *Sonnets* are the acme of poetic achievement anywhere, ever; and secondly, Jennifer Reeser is one of the handful of contemporary poets whom I judge to be the very best now writing — in earnest of which I have, as an editor of various literary journals, proudly published her work whenever I could get my hands on it. So it is not surprising that her collection entitled *Sonnets from the Dark Lady and Other Poems* has already commanded my full and enthusiastic attention even before I began to read it.

A major reason for my admiration of Reeser's work is that it has an unmistakably Elizabethan and Jacobean feel to it, deriving from the vigour and energy of her deployment of language, figure and image, the delight in word-play and verbal music, and the close personal engagement with addressed subject. The 'Other Poems' of the collection's title appeals to me for other reasons too of course: for example, its fertile links with French symbolism, channelled through a kind of Louisiana Gothic; and the authenticity of its passion. In both the 'Dark Lady' sequence and the 'Other Poems', shades of darkness are explored; 'black' (and near synonyms) is one of the most frequently used words.

The collection's title invites a degree of intertextualised reading which is sustained and justified, but also richly transcended, by the astonishing textual performance of the poems themselves, both individually and as a group. Various implied dramas behind the poems in this collection resonate with aspects of Shakespeare's Sonnets, especially of course the 'Dark Lady' sequence of sonnets 127 to 154; and in particular, Reeser weaves a complex, precisely passionate poetic discourse which gestures towards, but is not entirely contained by, a narrative suggesting rivalry in love, emblazoned with sensuous and chromatic imagery where binaries of darkness and light, *gris-gris* and *fleur de lis*, make subtle and elegant interplay; where shifting perspectives, unreliable narrators, masks and personae are set up, only (as in Shakespeare's *Sonnets*) to be subsequently subtly subverted. Yet from within this essentially tropical narrative matrix each individual poem can be detached and read as a text standing perfectly realized in its own right — but never falling into the comfortable slough of easy, stereotyped answers to whatever topic is being explored. On every structural level the poet's consummate formal technical skill, compositional vision, probing (and sometimes uncomfortable) poetic insights into human experience, individually brilliant elegances and sheer verbal and musical fluency flow together into an intricate choreography, a Masque of contemporary yet ancient poetic experience that serious readers of poetry will not want to miss.

Paul Stevens, editor of *The Chimaera, The Flea, SCR*

Gosford, New South Wales,

Australia

As Always

If I should die before I wake, I might.
The vital words are viable and spoken.
As always, you are in my prayers tonight.

The street outside my window seems too bright
sans moonlight, a reflection merely token
if I should die. Before I wake, I might

sleep restlessly without a little light
beneath the door, before you, too, are woken
as always you are – in my prayers. Tonight

the pillow in their path lies watertight,
the heart between its feathers still unbroken.
If I should die before I wake, I might:

The vital words are breathing and alright.
The vital words are viable and spoken.
As always, you are in my prayers tonight,

and I could give away the ghost, and spite
its going, knowing that your arms are open,
if I should die before I wake. I might,
as always. You are in my prayers tonight.

As Van Gogh Must Have Seen

Du passé lumineux recuielle tout vestige!
Charles Baudelaire, "Harmonie du Soir"

The sky is violet-olive with a hurricane.
Twelve feet of water delve to what was arid land.
And like six knuckles of the Deuce's knotted hand,
Distressing things are knocking at the windowpane.

Twelve feet of water delve to what was arid land.
Silk-tasseled tallows first to snap, the cypress strains.
Distressing things are knocking at the windowpane,
Wet pavement turned to palisades of playground sand.

Silk-tasseled tallows first to snap, the cypress strains,
One band of beatings followed by another band.
Wet pavement turned to palisades of playground sand,
Dual games of solitaire are going, while it rains.

One band of beatings followed by another band,
The card decks etched with phantoms, checks and chatelaines,
Dual games of solitaire are going, while it rains,
As unchecked waves wash up against a sea-walled strand.

The card decks etched with phantoms, checks and chatelaines,
As children paint toy plaster masks for contraband,
As unchecked waves wash up against a sea-walled strand,
Obscure doors opened on their own give one chilblains.

As children paint toy plaster masks for contraband,
You light a crystal lantern by what light remains.
Obscure doors opened on their own give one chilblains.
Why drafts revolve around you, you don't understand.

You light a crystal lantern by what light remains.
Why drafts revolve around you, you don't understand.
And like six knuckles of the Deuce's knotted hand,
The sky is violet-olive with a hurricane.

At the Crypt of Marie Laveau

As August closed the coffin on July,
I paid a visit to the voodoo queen
Beneath the omen of a grave vault sky.

The perfect afternoon for such a scene –
The atmosphere unusually stale,
A Sunday, with no crowds, and thus serene.
Unbroken gray had made the heavens pale,
Robbing the sun of every inch of room
Like doomed air from a Danish fairy tale.

Where else should I have sought her, but in gloom?
And yet no rain, nor any sense of dread
Surrounded me as I approached the tomb.

The roof rose in a plain block overhead,
Devoid of statuary, stone or crosses,
The dullest in this City of the Dead;
But that most found within a town of losses.

Across its base lay offerings: cologne
From Paris, garish beads and bayou mosses;
Sweets, carnival doubloons, a chicken bone,
Hydrangeas and foam cups with drinking straws,
Five-dollar bills, unfolded and wind-blown;
Elastic trinkets, plastic dime-store kickshaws,
Lead pencils with a blue-ink fountain pen,
What might have been a roll of bandage gauze.

Where were the givers of those tokens? When
Were they administered, and for how long
Would they remain? And who would have them then?
So many motives there – so many strong,
So many weak…were I to close my eyes,
Their afterimage might mix right with wrong.

Telling myself I must not empathize
Too much, become like one condemned, I leaned
Toward one wall, and let my shoulder rise,

Feeling with that motion like a fiend
Whom she had summoned with her incantations
Of shaman charm – contorted and un-cleaned.

And, too, amid the various oblations,
I felt like – convoluted and complex –
I were her native language in translation,

Intoning for every triple "X"
Etched on the stucco, prayers for her salvation,
A careful tear for every careless hex.

Bare Limbs, Three Black Birds
(Scenes from the Tempest)

One's view, conveyed through rain as this raid brews,
transmutes bamboo and grass blade to grayed bruise.

A sapling trunk. Spade-black wings cruise, three crows,
the space between them made a storm-sprayed bruise.

Nucleus of gnarled bark, there moves
A yew in wheeling breezes. Winds trade brews.

Numbering the branches, I count three –
a jubilant crucifix the fowl blades bruise.

Three thin, bare limbs – twigs at all ends – slipnoose
drab sky: dry, grabbing fingers that, splayed, bruise.

The few, enthusiastic neutrals soothe me
with loose tones while this cyclone's tirade brews.

Beneath confused blank boughs, ground gravels blend
in grainy coffee shale, like fine-grade brews.

Stiff, broomstick turf consumes the undergrowth
in pools of ragweed. Plunge, my prayers. Wade. Bruise.

His cruel, translucent eye proves coolly sage,
The maid of *Orléans* his jade to bruise.

Whose bare limbs are his nightshade, whose moods sluice
On brooding gravel through him? Abrade? Bruise?

This wild is Purgatory, fused and backed,
chalk-ruled by heaven, each line a white, flayed bruise.

If truth or tree should strike me in this gloom,
Would you bear my stigma in a blue, staid bruise?

I braid Kat's locks to news of latitudes
and lemon chamomile the kitchen-aid brews.

I lose my true name, choose, afraid, *Gustav* –
"God's staff" – and laugh. Clouds swirl, a burl-rayed bruise.

because the cut your presence

because the cut your presence is to ache
to ache {oh no one else no no one none}
but wooed so be it orderless so won
hello it means my half in heart you break
you break {but sweetly by and by mistake}
apart and and unhealing come undone
dearly departed dear but just begun
{so broken darling so: yours to remake}

since shrouds must shrouds be love be gone to bury
the cut hello that is goodbye and sad
if true minds not indeed admit to marry
{so faithful darling faithful} let me add
to we can't be and we can be together
go don't regardless what whenever whether...

Blind Concessions

*'The Sibyl, with frenzied mouth uttering things not to be laughed at,
unadorned and unperfumed, yet reaches to a thousand years
with her voice by aid of the god.'*
(Heraclitus, fragment 12)

Sightless Sybil at the pastry stand
wears white, and with a checkered terry towel
wipes down the counter with one wrinkled hand,
always a smile above her cardigan cowl.

I wonder if she's ever seen herself,
or if the sightlessness has lasted long
as her own life. How does she know each shelf
so well, each packet's bin or hanging prong
with such unerring swiftness and ballet?
A patron wouldn't guess the eyes are dead.

Her hair is scissored neatly – brief, pearl-gray,
tucked close as a cap around the oval head.

She trusts you to divulge the right amount
you've placed into her palm, pale wrists upturned
against the flecked, faux-granite of the board.
Are they, in business baking, ever burned?
Are *café noirs* or instants ever poured
onto the flesh?
        Because as motions go,
hers have the kind of clarity the seeing
could envy: that excess, that overflow
inherent in the bearing born of being.

Blue-Crested Cry

We're through, we're through, we're through, we're through,
we're through
and – flanking, now, the edges of our schism –
it seems your coldness and my idealism
alone for all this time have kept us true.

Credulous I and hedonistic you:
opposed, refracting angles of a prism
who challenged sense with childish skepticism –
and every known the bulk of mankind knew.

By This Pitch And Motion

In the upstairs hallway, complacent sunlight
stings the walls with gold and translucent almond
over Turkish runners betraying patterns
faded with travel.

At their raveled edges, my daughter slumbers
in the room from which this lost sun arranges
through a window high on an eastern sill of
drapes and black lacquer.

Past the pillowcase where her blonde head swivels
in a dream of chocolate, or paint and horses,
I imagined rest on the gingham, but it
proved only shadow...

Surely evening goes by this pitch and motion,
by the rasp of fans at the center ceiling,
and the purposes of an outside cypress
hidden from hearing.

But again it's day, in which dust turns static.
Almost blank of heart, I'll descend the staircase
with a babbled tune on the landing like a
passage to being.

The Charm of Candelabras

The charm of candelabras is unique,
old lace and arsenic adjoined, antique,

far-fetching on a shelf of formal sage –
though practical only in a previous age.

Arrange as you prefer: on serving boards
or china cabinets, under heirloom swords

passed down from generation to generation,
or picked up from Goodwills, the preservation

of which gives one a sense of heritage,
tradition, continuity, privilege.

Left on a level, four-inch window casement,
they'll burn the best, and if not, a replacement

is always to be found and had. The mind
reels at the newer versions it can find,

and much can be discerned about oneself
from lit wick dramas on a painted shelf,

representations in some magazine
archived with Cary on the silver screen;

that – for the one undazed and dagger-nerved –
in the end, will lighten brighter than deserved.

Civic Centre
(for Kathryn)

Moscow ballet at seven in the eve.
You look at everything. You lay your cheek
against my shoulder, smoothing down my sleeve,
the Russian blizzards somehow less than bleak,
portrayed with whimsy on the backdrop screens
in dolloped watercolors as they are.
I ask if you know what their movement means.
You wish our situation not so far.

And everywhere, the audience defies
convention and conformity, some dressed
as though they had been made to improvise
at the last minute, some in black-tie best.

You're happy, in new satin, having run
your fingers countless times from hip to hem –
Anastasia, whereas I am anyone
in tan, beside a jade and garnet gem.

With clarity and ease like these a-stage,
comparison with any else in life
seems but the smart annoyance of an age,
scissors beside a blunted paperknife.

"Sit up. Pay close attention. Sugar Plum
is dancing with such dignity," I tell
you, half-disheartened, when I hear you hum,
you know Tchaikovsky's symphony so well.

A Cockroach Wore His Sympathy

A cockroach wore his sympathy to dinner at *The Heather.*
(He claimed it was the warmest thing he owned, for chilly weather).
The day was wide with sunshine, the feelings were in flight.
The ladybug and katydid were livid with delight.
The cockroach cried, "I've come so far! I've crawled a country mile!"
The insects jeered, "You should have worn a more impressive style."
"We cannot feed a cousin whose clothing is so drab,
But you may stay and entertain, if you've the gift of gab."
Each place was laid with chiseled care, with silver, china, linen;
The loud cicadas hushed in awe, the water bugs were spinnin'.
Each plate was heaped with turnip greens, with dew and honey-mud,
And each mosquito gorged himself on sparkling, scarlet blood.
The cockroach gazed politely at a root-and-blossom pie,
Then buttoned up his sympathy, and smiling with a sigh,
Said, "Think! I might have joined them, if my suit were just more queer!"
He brushed away a bit of lint as lissome as a tear.
The insects slurped each stamen dry; they quite disturbed the cherries.
They chuckled as they finished off the helpless chinaberries.
"How fortunate," a cricket chirped, "we are not like the beasts
Who show such bad behavior as to belch at first-rate feasts!"
Then when they'd chewed the table bare of each delicious thing,
A love-bug climbed the roach's back, and led them all to sing,
"The strategy of swallowing! The science, how it tickles
To gorge, to gulp the purest plums, demean the greenest pickles!
How elegant, to dine and drool, until our napkins float!"
With that, the moths shook down the roach, and ate his winter coat.

Considering Dolphins

A dolphin of a kind, I contemplate
Their constant noising by some click or whistle
Too high for human ears: that sonar missile
With which, obscure and sleek, they navigate;
And how, through humor, they affiliate,
Disarming sharks and mines, and of the gristle
Making distinctly signature each dorsal;
And the human speech they may approximate;
The totem for our counselors and sages,
Insignias for princes, who adapt
Too swiftly to aquariums in cages –
So quick to the performance, so enrapt
To play themselves for little-to-no wages,
As though uniqueness were a periapt.

Corner Memorials

Cobwebs are gentle companions - suspended
judgments from corners ill-suited to business -
likely to quake at the easiest breezes.
Making such manners of white, they appear as
softer for being abandoned addresses;
never wind-weary, in love, never conscious of death;

always the archives of spiders forgotten,
dusted profoundly with age, but annoying
gravity - heavy, without the mundane or
motions too grand for a commonplace corner.
So I preserve them, where no one's the wiser -
watching their abstracts to sullen, self-occupied air,

only to honor the child who once, somewhere,
walked a wood ribboned with live webs of creatures
eager to welcome his cheek with eight legs till,
somewhere, a wiser one stopped him before his
face hit the sticky sheet without decorum --
then moved away through the silence that followed,
leaving behind him a web I've enshrouded with time.

The Crooked Cookie House

Fiends of whipped vanilla and seafoam frosting
hover high and bloated at upper windows
where, for stained glass, triangle candy corn sticks,
pasted with sugar.
Burnt and scattered coconut flakes for landscape,
warping, nougat gourds nudge against a fencing
sketched with dull fudge -- sloppy, be-smudged and jagged
halberd-topped ground poles.
Every pastry-slender partition is coated,
slight, but thorough. Licorice doorways hinging
creak to cream, the marshmallow-bloodless moth balls
hide in gum powder.
Its repulsive artistry smells of ginger,
which we name -- despite a stark, Salem spirit --
the decrepit, glamorous Hotel Gold Rush,
north California.
It's our 13 *Rue Street* of seven gables,
shingled thick with icing and purple fruit pearls
for a fall of ushers: the chill air shift,
the shadows prolonging.
One could even picture within the foyer
native shades defying the decoration
on the tense facades of its troubled shutters
eavesdropping syrup.
Mannered cats are there, but with common whiskers,
gelid-jointed skeletons addle-basking
not in morgue fluorescence, nor orange flame,
but natural sunlight.

And the wax-museum-like, jelly cellars
weren't designed for torture, but hanged obsessions
of an unaccountable baseness -- iron
maidens of cocoa.
Could its walls convince us that they are sentient,
would we walk away? Or become caretakers,
adding family plots to the backyard garden,
loyal through horror?

Deepwater Horizon Oil Spill in the Gulf of Mexico

Each day by twenty thousand cruder counts
of oil, our Gulf becomes a new Black Sea
alike to state and science, who pronounce
this eruption our worst well in history.

What algebraic voodoo now may we
summon by some drilling of the moon
to choke the concupiscence of a zombie,
a real, real creature of a black lagoon?

I feel I and my statesmen must exist
in order to provide our country's neighbors
with more of substance, so the optimist
may rest with more content in boring labors,

or sate an appetite for the dramatic,
perhaps safe space in which to ruminate.
Storms and blasts have left a vapid attic
for our recovery, a room's-full to abate

this jerking, as if we are side-stepping crabs
in iridescent pools of lifeless shrimp,
through currents like retractable morgue slabs –
beach agues where the grouse and egret limp.

Evening Harmony
By Charles Baudelaire

Here coming is the time when on its stem will blow
Each flower, like a censer, now evaporating.
The sounds and the perfumes turn in the air of evening,
A melancholy waltz and languid vertigo!

Each flower, like a censer, now evaporating,
The violin is quivering like a heart in woe,
A melancholy waltz and languid vertigo!
The sky is sad and lovely, like a great repose.

The violin is quivering like a heart in woe,
A tender heart, which hates vast, black oblivion!
The sky is sad and lovely, like a great repose.
The sun is drowned in its own blood which thickens.

A tender heart which hates vast, black oblivion
Collects all vestiges from bygone luminance!
The sun is drowned in its own blood which thickens...
Your remembrance shone within me like a monstrance!

The Eye Passes

Disturbing skies, and in the dark a frightening
howling of the wind through banging blinds.
You raise the rattling window; moisture grinds
against the screen within a bolt of lightning.
The dawn's far off – before it, a deluge
will come, *must* come: there is a heady price
for balancing the brink of paradise
here in the sultry smirk of Baton Rouge.
The winds may be demolishing your walls;
the awnings from their porticoes released
as someone strange pronounces you deceased
and high gusts shriek in intermittent squalls.
You may not realize until too late
water is rising to your upper floors,
the knobs of antique crystal on your doors –
discreet, hand-sculpted keyhole, silver plate
submerged as any solemn cypress knee.
Pecan limbs hung with bags of reptile leather
or beads from past parades, entwined together
with seafood ads and signs for local tea
are things you'll start to recognize as apt.
A funnel cloud, not wholly there but forming,
will drop, then disappear, the meters warming.
Black coffee in your cup becomes white-capped.
Soundest of attitudes will seem insane;
your books will page to pieces on their shelves;
pine shutter slats make music by themselves,
as you embrace and curse the hurricane.

Despair

She's not the special one you thought
would need protection till the end.
She licks up quarrel when it's fraught
with rude clichés meant to offend.
You have conceived and borne a whore
who won't defend you, on her bed.
Eve's fruit – sweet juice and rancid core –
she leaves you, with a bobbing head,
to rot in barrelfuls of water
you'll dump, as she sneaks off to play.
She is your one and only daughter,
who used to spread in every way
on nursery walls her tot's manure.
And you will die, once she's mature.

It Seems Your Speech

It seems yours is a speech I'll never master –
A rich, occult air spilled from sacred lungs
Like worship in a church in which the pastor
Continually chants in other tongues.
A sympathetic showing of the word
Would be sufficient edifice, although
Confusion in attendance feels absurd.
When no interpretation comes, I go.
Some deity of clay is ever toying
With my opinions, balance, comprehension.
I cannot tell you which is more annoying –
Your "vastness," or the slivered condescension
To be endured, hiding what I hear
But disagree with, lest *it* sound unclear.

Fire Mount

Very in love, not leveling love very well,
I thrust a trowel, throw pepper, hoe and tell

How like a hill whose growth I can't retard
Of ants, gray and aggressive in the yard,

It thrives: of even and its own volition.
My pesticides break down to superstition –

Original yet olden to observe
As the bold bore of long-told proverb.

When soil with poison in addition can't
Eradicate the raisings of the ant,

At least one can admire the bitten pin-
Round boil it raises on a dirty shin,

So like a pristine pearl, that oyster bead
Resulting from a nearly fatal seed.

What if one found such things inside the pile?
 Some precious ball designed of brawn and bile,

A polished billiard for their going nation
Built on the industry of irritation?

Preferred – but never banking in these fires
Does one disclose those brokerage desires.

The carcass of a swallow or canary
Alongside their production line, one very,

Very in love, not balancing its bite,
Must powder the mound with talc, then smother the site.

For The Haunted Child

The circles underneath your violet eyes
remain with me once I have closed my own.
I know those ghosts the nightlight will disguise.
I've seen the starkness in the half-starved bone,
the straining candor and the skittish grace,
and all too well the spell of feverish care
falling across the laughter in your face
when she descends the last step on the stair.
Such is the quinine of the quiet nurse.
One day, we have, of hide-and-seek and verse.
I cannot keep you ever sheltered, mold you
according to what I think love should be.
One afternoon is all I have to hold you,
hoping it is enough to keep you free.

Formula

In the absence of a basement,
A dry attic will suffice
To hide beneath some casement
Damning evidence of vice.

A blunder cannot lurk too much.
Drawers were made for errors:
The bludgeoned bunny in its hutch,
Botched marriage and block terrors.

Dead bats, however, in your books
May mean mystique and fame –
A secret hung from rusting hooks;
And title for one's name
Is gotten – whether earned or dubbed
By crowds, events or seasons.

If by some accident you've flubbed
Your latest strange malfeasance,
Repair upstairs to ghosts and geese
Of gypsum. Breathe in drought,
Guarding as it were the peace
Gossips will chit about.

French Quarter Singer

Strumming your polished guitar with long, nail-lightened fingers,
where are you now, leaning forward a peasant-dressed arm –
lark on the near side of midnight, my crescent curb lady,
ear to your sound, dangling each with a silver folk charm?
Sweet was your voice for an evening, amid the brash jazzy –
seamless soprano, your scales a tough, platinum thread.
Angel on brick, tipping jar at your feet, were you happy
smiling at me through the blonde of your half-hanging head?
Monies I dropped in its opening I have forgotten.
Doubtless you spent them with virtue as pure as your song.
And if you didn't, no damage, oh cantor of sugar:
Fair was your all for one night. You will keep my love long.

Gentle Country

Give me the traveled, exploited, the used,
something in suffering from triumph or toil.
I have no interest in land unabused,
nor do I lust after rough, virgin soil.

I am offended that Man can abandon
so much he's conquered, once novelty goes –
thus came the reflex, to shelter the tendon;
thus came the thorn, for protecting the rose.

There is no need of new ground to arrest me.
Callousness thrives on the conqueror's hands.
Magic and evidence both have addressed me.
I have preferred what the heart understands.

Something baroque in me seeks the ripped wallpaper,
loves the singed carpet, the sandblasted door –
leading me through the old hallway, the hall-vapor,
telling me, *Touch. Smooth. Recover. Restore.*

Halloween Queen of Hearts

At Halloween, I'll play the Queen of Hearts,
With steamed *café au lait*, cream *à la carte*
And crushed pecan-nut pralines. Creole arts.

She'll have no hand to hold, though I, her host,
Will haunt with hospitality her most
High-rolled and age-old hairbreadth : a good ghost.

And while her roses – red with English fable
Harass as they are shuffled on the table,
Not folding, I shall focus on her sable;

For all my focus, failing to devise
A way to represent her outlined eyes:
Four, shifting shut – framed, lashing dragonflies.

Double-faced but flat, she will behave
Beside a sharp-set jack, that handbill knave
Vainglorious in tarts and aftershave.

If, by position, he suggests that she
Is hypocritical, or cowardly,
Or dumb with detail, I should then agree.

My intention being as it is to weave
Her dress to wear, her hallmark on my sleeve,
I'll drop his comments, though, that Hallows Eve,

Believing when the cards are cut a bit,
My foolishly affected hypocrite
Will shrive the cutting hand, not shirk from it.

Harlequins by Hurricane Lamp

Pipe-like, in scarlet suit, noble expression,
next to Pierrot, Cézanne would depict him.
Belted with thin suede, Paul's harlequin poses,
foil to the white clown's pale, humble impression –
bowing, one hand at the jester's red elbow.
Mardi Gras, he would entitle the scene.

Gazing and blank, stiffly set on a chair
sketched with tasseled proviso, Picasso would render
one formal child in their costume – a tender,
somber tableau of blue, triangled yellow:
Sad Gala's Son, an ethereal fellow;
all but his feet finished – Harlequin's heir.

Cézanne and Picasso would paint them with feeling.
Always, my own grace a wall of some bedroom,
quilted in jaundice-and-jet-jacket diamonds,
casting their masked gazes up to the ceiling,
stylishly sulking for childish amusement,
set in a glassless, wood octagon frame.

Fate disallowing them gender or name,
sexless as angels mine stand, in full stocking,
porcelain-simple, dimpled and mocking,
solitaire – paired with a lone, fallen ribbon,
kitten or onion, brush-stroked on a background
mottled with ochres or motley matte tans.

Eyes so enormous, they stand as Fate stands:
sure and old-fashioned, mysterious, modern.
"Faith in me?" closes their confident question.

Hardest of all to depict are the hands.
Theirs remain hidden, both arms hung behind them.
Distant, invisible things never fail.
Wizened clowns…Under some pear tree with quail,
clear and Medieval, their hands to the pheasant,
I wish for their names, uttered low in a setting
merry and modernized, modest emotion
etched in wan faces – forgiving, forgetting.

Her Feet

"Take off your shoes," he chuckles when they meet,
Glasses on, to hide his rural glance,
"And nylons – let me see those perfect feet,"
A bent towards dereliction in his stance.

He claims it is her high and compact arch,
The first two toes' precisely matching height,
Imagining her barefoot in a marsh,
Vulnerable to asp and insect bite.

Persistently, embarrassingly pointed,
He presses her – now raw, now sentimental:
Christ's own disciples' feet not so anointed,
Nor more adored the cloth-bound Oriental.

To her, however, (resolute romantic),
Suspicious of the slyly sensual,
The overtures seem vainly automatic,
The mannerisms ever casual.

He's restless, and while she can empathize,
Assiduous and diligent to please,
She keeps each foot tucked in its snug high rise,
Her laces tied completely. She foresees

Herself upon some summer afternoon
On an ottoman squatting on a shopfront floor
With russet walls and carpets of maroon,
Before a boy upon his knee, before

A boy who – loyal salesman – takes her heel,
And murmurs, *in our back room, there is more…;*
Whose livelihood's afoot, his impulse real,
Sincerely earned in this poor, family store.

Hestia

For all men's worship, I would not have war,
Nor give Pandora's jar for any god.
Two suitors in pursuit of me, and each
Infinity to reach – what they could do…
I am Poseidon's dolphin, it is true.
Although his eyes are not so blue, I care
To watch him dare – for my fidelity –
A contest with Apollo. I oppose
The taunt, the prick, the chartreuse spill of ichor
That poisons all the red of human flesh
Which mimics our "inspiring" undertakings.
O Father, do you not suppose I see
Into whose care I'd go, in either case?
We are of one mind, Zeus, and I will swear
Upon your brow, as though it were my own.
You ask how I will answer faithlessness.
Your warnings do not pierce through ears of pearl.
I am no mortal girl, to let the heart
Enshroud the head with killing sentiments.
I need no show of history to know
Blonde Aphrodite's ways would dwindle me.
What offspring I obtained from either union –
Apollo or Poseidon for a sire –
Would not mature, forever being infants,
Adding their stunted stories to our legends,
Their failures through combined naivete
With steel rebellion, and a trace of malice.
Once I renounce them, will you comfort me?
Grant sanctuary for me, from those sobs
Which rob the lover's chest of its gold breath?
My prayer is for myself for now, but after

For all; my altar made for amnesty,
Asylum for a home within myself,
A kettle at my ankle, purple iris
For weaving into crowns for sacred sows.
Perhaps not glamorous as Hera's peacock,
Nor circumspective as Athena's owl,
But crucial, notwithstanding, to the City.
Grant me a plain white throne, white woolen cushions
And if I chose a cult, who would they be?
Twelve, virginal, to love and honor me.
Exempt from haste, but quick to colloquy,
And privy to all secrets of the State.
Great trust is granted to the greatly chaste.
Among the common, give my congregants
Choice seats between the singular and strong.
They quit adventure, pardon the accused,
Preserve the fire. They hold their own, unowned,
Immovable as hearthstone, and as lone
As flame; of virtue, a residuary
For Rome, for Greece, Europa...for the world.
And if or when such sisters fall, that fall
Must come from such exalted heights, its force
Will bury them alive. Give me your word.
Protect me by your power on my way.
Approaching Sun and Ocean, I will say,
"Let us be friends, Poseidon, intimates,
If you allow. Apollo, let me be
Perpetuating Essence, Untouched Core –
And ask no more than these, for I have chosen
A task of tar and coal, to kindle daily,
Through cold observance, love from nothingness.

How I Want You

In white – a complimentary robe, with wine,
Eighteen floors skyward, on an armless chair
In some sub-tropical hotel, your hair
Damp as you're coming, fingers twined in mine;
Before you on my knees – but not in prayer;

With blanket views of pink and black flamingoes
Below us on the gravel going south
Eighteen flights down, my lips, my tongue and mouth
In speech that leaves you with a speechless groan,
The *sotto* strains of Pinzas and Domingos,
Dvořáks, brought to silence, speakers blown;

My right sole on an air conditioner
Beside our still-untumbled, unturned bed
Against clove-papered walls, your dripping head
Between my hips: the plosive connoisseur
Exploiting, lecture justified and deft,
As though you tasted sweet, concocted salve.
And I, I am escaping like I have
Nothing undiscovered in me left.

Then on the rented floor, a *fleur-de-lis* –
Silver and subtle – pending from my throat
In motion over you, a cunning coat
Of sweat between your cradling joints and me.

Inviolate and sacred I am not,
But cleaving, suckling, bringing you for good
Inside thin garter bands and thigh-high leggings,
Recalling practice tacit Rome forgot
In Ilium's abandoned vestal wood
By acquiescence and ignoble begging.

The pendant catching sun, then moonlight, dangles
Atop our rocking. *Oh, my love*, you say.
My feet are bare, the carpets hard to heel.
The room contains an endless count of angles,
And I want you – how I want you – any way
The reason can conceive, or heart can feel.

I love you as I love night's sepulcher...
By Charles Baudelaire

I love you as I love night's sepulcher,
O vase of sadness, grand and taciturn,
And love you more, my belle, that you take flight,
And seem to me, adornment of my nights,
Ironically gathering the space
Which keeps blue vastnesses from my embrace.

I make advance, I mount to my assault,
Like a chorus of worms to a corpse within the vault,
And I cherish, o creature cruel and still!
Your beauty, made the greater by this chill!

If We're To Make This Work

For Heaven's sake, don't say you wear a tie
and sip black coffee on your way to work;
that you were once the pride of Sigma Chi,
and even friends acknowledge you're a jerk;
don't ever swear to me your eyes are blue,
that you prefer your hair and nails clipped short,
Professor Plum was always yours for *Clue*,
and you don't keep a girl in every port.
And never, *ever* tell me you hate cats,
(especially the grey and ugly tabbies),
or that on weekends you wear baseball caps
and hiking boots, and interact with cabbies,
leave dirty water standing in the sink,
or think of me, or care what I may think.

In Days to Come

Remembering me, philosophic, sober,
you will forgive my cruder attitudes,
to focus on my birthday in October,
or love for Degas' after-bathing nudes.

When lived, elapsed, and muted are my weeks
of galling negligence, you will recall
Cezanne's still lifes of pitchers paired with leeks
or Claude Monet's train stations on my wall.

And -- thanking God that I am gone -- you'll think,
Good glory, what a flecked and sketchy wench,
most every tack about her black or pink,
Ming Dynasty, chinoiserie or French.

A winter storm will stripe the sky with gray,
when you will be reminded how I swore
Renoir's striped dame and boating *déjeuner*
would look forever on my dining floor;

Bonnard, Vuillard the Intimists, determine
my blue *boudoir* beside a gold-scrolled sconce;
my study keep its *Portrait with an Ermine* --
da Vinci's lady of the Renaissance.

What unicorns and gryphons I collected
in youth! To be replaced by these mundane
commodities of nature – though excepted
and rare, if marred by an infrequent stain.

Artistic angst with vital glamour vanished
like sere impressionists to pop up daisies,
my blotted presence may turn out a banished
resemblance of small muses to great mazes.

In the House of Disguises

Paneled walls adorned with masks:
Spanish, African, from Venice,
some a comfort, some a menace –
all a master craftsman's tasks.
Glassy hurricane lanterns glow,
raised on shelves or ceiling grooves,
hooks. The makers' skill improves
further towards the back you go.
Peacock plumes or batwing edges
feather blithely, as you brush
past the difficult and lush
miniature French terrace ledges
used as masquerader props.
Black Arachne bares her canines;
Pan, Anubis, woman-felines,
sprites or grinning lollipops
swing from zombie walnut cases,
cueing – through their dingy portal –
visions of the vague immortal;
Time defied by timeless faces.
Sniffling faintly, frail and plump,
fair, the shopgirl tells you tales.
Counter to the room, she pales –
quick, in its dim joy, to jump.
Oh, to reach out boldly, take
hold, and veil in silver leaf!
Harshness here is bas relief,
Pathos all for Pathos' sake.

Half the native bravery
one needs to angle forth and grasp,
saps into each jack and asp.
European revelry,
never so distinctly felt,
leaves you open, leaves you only –
half in love with lovely, lonely
poltergeists of card and Celt.

Instructions for the Cemetery Cake

(from "Grave Nursery Rhymes")

To make a cemetery cake,
first wash your hands, then take and break
rotten eggs into a powder lake;
pour in black sugar, blend and bake.

Be sure the oven heat devours
its outer crust and burns the flours.
Allow it afterward for hours
to cool in dampness till it sours.

Assemble spatulas, and ice
the top with grass green salt. Drop rice
for gravel pathways where the nice
bereaved may mourn – one man per slice.

Lining Up for the Tower of Terror
(Walt Disney World, 2007)

Grouped by long queues in a windowless basement,
Standing on slab ramps of rigorous, mellow
Gray, between rails sprayed industrial yellow,
Eager and damp as sardines, wait the damned.

One floor above, an elaborate mansion –
Dim with nostalgia – grows into a tower
Twelve stories high, a Victorian vision
Stained but familiar the damned are awaiting
Thrilling ascent through, in new elevators.

Unlearned but curious, lonely and loud,
Shod with flat rubber soles, shudders the crowd.
Tall and gaunt bellhops attend them in crimson,
Packing them – friendless and coupled alike –
Into their journey.
           A paltry elect
Reaching the end of the line circumspect,
Shortly reluctant to ride now, faint-featured,
Opt for an exit, before the last call.

Led by some lone, extra bellhop to safety,
Looking back once at their fellows aligning
Plot-coded squares for the imminent lift,
Those who escape are grape phantoms.
                They sift
Strangely through tunnels, and past the grate vents,

Back to the affluent drawing room entry
Grounded with woolens, a tin-armor sentry
Grasping its halberd, exact at their fringe.

Outside it's raining, the gates slicked with drizzle,
Spanish moss spooking the willow leaf oaks.
Hear the mortality hush their discussions
Down to the creep of a hesitant drawl,
Braking their pace to a parking lot crawl,
Far beyond fear, and high-priced, fizzing cokes.

Jackson Square, Sunday Morning

Criminals splintered a shop front
Saturday night in the rain,
lifting its hinge from the casements,
warping both glasses and grain.

Roaming the alleys in grayness,
early I saw it, and saw
smashed avocadoes on pavement,
ices beginning to thaw.

There was a store on the corner
bordered with mauve, its façade
lilac, Victorian, angled,
tall – several-storied – and odd.

Up to that hour, I'd been happy
not to be bothered by scenes:
cameras snapping their pictures,
ironwork, aquamarines.

Skies were an optic of eggshell,
uninterrupted November.
Suddenly I wanted portrait –
something from truth to remember.

The Key to Hippocratic Evasion

I've been a Melancholy female since Day One and prone
to draw the offhand, upbeat, downtown Sanguine male -- unknown
until too late, most times. (*You* know: *Ve vant to be alone...*)

First there was Glenn the Bright, who chased me round a cattail bog,
apparently thinking me the princess, he my fated frog.
I found a tree. He found the molars of my best friend's dog.

I'll skip the more complex evasions, but suffice to say
I used to envy Atalanta's savvy getaway,
and Artemis's trick, as well - no girl too good to spay.

But I was so naive! It's taken all these years to see -
(Hippocrates! Where were you in my maiden *bourgeoisie?*)
the best defense was lighter-apperceptioned repartee.

Pursued had been pursuer in the batting of an eye
with Dave, who flipped up collars but forgot to zip his fly,
and thought himself a *tour-de-force*, because his jokes were dry.

"The proper study of mankind is man," Pope told us all.
My great advice to unrequiting loves is: find a mall
that sells your nemesis's traits. Feign phlegm. Feign blood. Feign gall.

The goal's to find a personality assured to weary
your suitor's own, and render him appropriately leery --
though, if you rival Helen, this may stoke things. It's a theory.

But think of the advancements to be had for womankind
if each evasive would-be would be cruel to be kind!
Or maybe this is irony.   I can't make up my mind.

Lady Grey

Lady Grey is called by the kitchen kettle
from her box of bergamot tea. Steam flushes
past the paste-and-canvas tomatoes and the
burgundy blushes.

Plates from Ives & Currier flank the trademarks:
Irish, China Pearl, and discreet mulberry.
Prince of Wales is missing, and Oolong, and with them
fragile Queen Mary;

steeped, then shed through ice is champagne Darjeeling
from some humble height in the Himalayas.
But who was this Lady of old, among her
earls and soothsayers?

Did she care for crinolines? Was she handsome?
Were her sense and silhouette slight or ample?
Did she lead by decree, or did she rather
lead by example?

What were her securities, disappointments?
Did she love to donate but loathe to borrow?
Was she too familiar, or too conforming?
What was her sorrow?

I would know, and could be complaisant knowing –
hold my tongue, allowing the tin to whistle
as I trimmed the fat from the lamb, accepting
grace with the gristle.

The Lady Who Lives Here

The lady who lives here is horribly vain.
Her mirrors are many, a mess to maintain.
She freezes, uneasy whenever they change.
The lady who lives here is strange.
She buys big sunglasses that look like bug lenses,
and bottles of cream meant for mane and tail rinses.
The lady who lives here loves fences.
She won't cook with wheat. All she uses is rice.
She won't keep a cat. She prefers to have mice.
She claims cats are cruel, with too-devilish eyes.
The lady here shuns the sun's rise.
She won't stay at parties for more than half-hours.
She really likes baths, but she always takes showers.
She turns sickly sweet, if a visitor sours.
She pretends to have deep, secret powers.
Her powders of proteins for skin, tooth and nail
she keeps in a cabinet until they go stale
with Halloween candy she's ordered on sale.
She's thin, with long arms, and too pale.
The lady who lives here -- oh, what can be said?
She has a black teddy and hare by the bed
and a black sheep she sleeps with. She never wears red,
only rose and magenta instead.
You'd see, if you stared through her weird windowpane
over dried flies, the flowers her vases contain.
She'll sort them and sort them, and then re-arrange.
The lady who lives here is strange.

Line to Circle

Willing to be disfavored on the theme
Of well-maintained restraint as it applies
To those I venerate, the things I prize,
And all priorities I most esteem,
Like a straight stroke within an artist's scheme
Of ovals – apt to few, unfit in size
Or scale, a fork where generally lies
A French curve – I will form the stern extreme.
Too much extended clarity of arc
Exists as yet in you, my friend, to end
A lenient, rolling vagrancy and talk,
And toward your widespread, catenary mark
From birth my temperament was meant to bend –
A charcoal shaft against a shield of chalk.

Litany

Wafers I hate, and champagne, and the shore
  on overcast days when the beach is bleak,
the jellyfish, manta and man-of-war
  washed up on the strand with the crooked teak
of the driftwood; chocolate chip cookies and chairs
  made out of vinyl, metals that rust
or copious woods. I hate silverfish, stairs
  without banisters…restlessness, sloth, wanderlust.

Man-made fabrics I hate, in coarse overblown plaids;
  fuschia, oatmeal-flecked granite and shrill smoke alarms.
Wafers I hate, and bizarre diet fads,
  and the thought of my love in another one's arms.

Mark My Words

I'll dress in black, walk out in widow's weeds –
consoling, and yet always unconsoled –
hang a creased flag of purple, green and gold
from Carnival, three strands of polished beads
around my throat. I shall repeat the creeds –
yes, each profession I was ever told –
prefer the night's oblivion and cold,
hold high a beribboned mask, evince no needs.

If then you swear you love me, I'll believe
forever or not once. I cannot say.
Perhaps I have no great desire to know.
I know my greatest comfort is to grieve,
that none should seek a graveyard in decay
as much as I, nor God in darkness so.

Millenium Park

Pressed clover on the picnic bench;
a miserable crew I've left behind;
my love with a nasty, bookish wench –
these are the tidings in my mind.

Three honeybees in unmown grass –
too slight, I think, and thin and long.
It's sunny here, without the crass,
chaotic, cross, or simply wrong,
and there are children's choruses, clear
as porcelain – a tire, a swing,
historic oak. And nothing here
unfitting to the break of spring.

Arched baby's breath and bridal wreath;
wisteria is nowhere found,
but wished for, on the iron teeth
of fencing round the picnic ground;
gray lilac, cool as dainty bells
in tint, in cluster frail enough.

The children shuffle through dense shells,
scraping the smooth against the rough.
Wisteria, light as fragile grape…
What clever phrases, thoughts profound
I might have penned just now escape
me – vanish. What an empty sound.

Minor Sonnet

Make these the measures in a minor key
you conjure when your drawing room grows blurred
with flawing daylight and you want a word
for measures played of pain; a strain in G –
what Mozart deemed the key of tragedy:
Vivaldi's *Winter*, or Frost's minor bird.

Your love vain coda, and your life absurd,
with Handel's small sonata on, these be
the verses yawing as you meditate
on lachrymose Fantine, the Brothers Grimm,
Chopin's *Nocturne*, Bach's Little Fugue, some beam
of Ludwig's *Moonlight*, pecked and desolate.

Make this the distich to a heart-sick hymn,
a requiem of meaning for a dream.

The Murderess

Gentlemen, not one warm ounce of saving blood
remained within my attitude that night.
With such warm approbation did he speak
of her, it was as if a stream had gushed
with gravity and furor to my feet
in one putrescent rush, against my will.
Against my will, believe me – please remember,
I was the ward of celebrated men.
Picture it – evening quasars shining queerly
outside the restaurant glass, on every side
around him as he spoke, his flat reflection
minutely moving in the candlelight:
her pedigree, her purity, her polish...
Imagine, too, I ask you to imagine –
if that is approved, in your prerogative –
the horror of pacific disposition
made hostage to reprising jealousy.
God. God! To be dismissed by one's own flesh,
no cogent pulse upon which sense might rest.
Each bleak insinuation of his voice –
his peerless voice – each operatic smile
weak cyanide, turning the olive hue
of my complexion green to baleful blue.
I ripped the linen and excused myself
to ladies' rooms and lilac-bordered mirrors,
where rude reality is viewed through filters,
but even those refused to shock my heart.
A banshee I'd become, as you have heard:

"Hell hath no fury," gentlemen. You see,
the noxious dead know torture, and a woman
discarded may maintain at pace with these.
Devotion not redressing, she exacts
her payment from the purses of her rivals.
Innocuous, essential, nearly wholesome –
my "subsidy" upon the stupid Earth –
seems Death to me, in reconsideration.
Forgive me then, but without charity,
and with no second chances. Even now,
I feel the chuck of slitting that slim throat
which made him so punch-drunk, and I was charmed
seeing her blood expounded, beat unchecked
across my breast and shoulders. I embraced her
as one would brace a child, as if her pulse
could start my heart again, and I am calmed
even now to know that pulse wastes in the ground.
And if she should return – the world is wide,
so hurry, sirs, to set my lock in stone –
I know my lover's voice, his mind, his stride.
Should she so much as wink, I won't think twice.

The Night Without

This night without your touch, this night alone,
this night of only hours and black on black,
runs out ahead of me: a metal track
through blowing weeds and blinding monotone.
I hear a distant whistle and the groan
of straining steel on steel, I feel the clack
of slats in motion with the shifting slack
of rotting grooves and rivets, hear the drone
of locusts fade away – just so much grief –
and conjure the deep solace of your voice
against the traffic and the scuttling leaf
unable to console me with their noise,
and wait, as though it counted if it be
minutes or years – or each the same to me.

Noli Me Tangere

"...for Caesar's I am,
And wild for to hold, though I seem tame. "
Sir Thomas Wyatt, *Whoso List to Hunt*

Yet I must stiffen on paved stone, and stare
Through lowered lashes, rigid at attention –
A priory hind who must not ever mention
In passion or respect distress or care;
While with a stance of disavowal there
Before me in blindsided apprehension,
You snap, you joke, to circumvent the tension
Of this ascetic pose. But if I dare
Deliberately deliver with a croak
Weak oaths, small sobs, suppose I'm making music,
Wild only by comparison to some.
Suppose I sing you hymns, instead of choke,
Intrepid in travail, un-trapped, not tragic,
And that my eyes are lifted, and not plum.

In These Photographs, My Rival

…grips a tapered wine glass, nearly drained,
Beneath a gold band and engagement gem;
Ham-fisted, left-hand fingers round the stem,
Forefinger lifted, fattened with the strain.
The symptoms of her sloe-eyed pose are pained,
Her lips pulled wide and reddened. Under them,
The edges of her V-dart collar hem
Conceal, almost, the goblet. Golden-veined
In theme, the lavish suite behind her speaks
Of debts and delegations fit for kings,
Troubadour orchestras, prime execution,
Absolute power and official leaks.
The velvet of its jetty panels sings
Of *coups d'etat,* Rousseau and revolution.

And here, in this, she wears true blue, couture
In polished rayon, modernist in flair
And line; the padded shoulders – broad and square –
Fall through long arms, thigh-level, too obscure
For fair description – lowered in demure,
Meek relaxation. Glossed and dense, her hair
Falls to the bijou throat's transcendence, bare
Of ornament: off-parted, insecure.
She seems anatomy immune to force:
Before her, ceremony and applause,
Behind and after nothing, barren space.
Be gratified, but warned, Self: in due course,
These hues will clash and die, those classic jaws,
The tongue that teased for hours a lover's face.

But even death, her ghost, won't bring you ease.
Some cranny of the house, some corner room,
Will be conscripted as a waking tomb
In which her soul is stored and made to freeze
Or swell by disproportionate degrees.
Her wardrobe, willow china, her perfume,
Initialed stationery – each assume
Precedence to your flawed, impassioned flesh;
A mothball take on mystical allure
Where you will be the spider in a welt
Above her bookshelf, spinning out your mesh
In mortal coiling, cloistered and impure,
Your webbing clogged with pastry cloth and felt.

What's Really Wrong

Admit it: what disturbs you isn't flaws
within the grand design, not that or this
ironic fealty to effect and cause
within the cosmic lottery. Dismiss
the phony, brief, and adolescent shock
at guns *in terra pax*, torrential rain
leveling every last cultivated block –
phlegmatic and dispassionate. The pain
of dull prevention is your sorrow's source.
By that which reputations circumvent
facile degeneration on its course,
along with sag and setback and descent,
observe brute effort. Look at it and weep.
Admit it. Flip the page. Go back to sleep.

On The Anniversary of A Natural Disaster

I found an infant alligator floating
in Perkins' Bayou yesterday, between
Louisiana iris and the green
of blighted summer reeds, its stomach bloating
with harsh, bright, glaring sunlight, without fault
or scale, as crocodiles would have; its head
chin up and oblong, grimacing, as dead
as mausoleum marble, white as salt.
Delight in a discovery so exotic
could not be lost on me, however grim.
Mosquito larvae harbored in a scrim
of water on the western bank, hypnotic
and circling with the rise-and-falling rasp
of locusts at the cypress. In my grasp
a camera – in the case some killer storm
destroys this haunt tomorrow, everything
familiar, safe, replaced by suffering –
chaos projecting fatally through form.

Prima Donna

She'll slash a dress for spite
With operatic shears
In fingers free from tears
If she's not given white
Lamé instead of gold –
No matter that it's tissue,
Opals in every fold.

Her complexion is at issue,
And gold lamé will clash
With braids of Viking ash,
and eyes of arctic brown.

She'll be no trouser clown
Performing tricks, a mask
With fluff of guinea hen
And rickrack at her chin.

She'll be sole, lyric bride –
Not prostitute, not whore,
Courtesan, paramour;

Who saw the other side
Of ticket, stage and tomb –
Coiled, red-faced, swollen, nude,
Unborn with attitude –
And exited the womb.

Proposal

If you have thought of me as much as I
have thought of you, then we are not alone.
Exhausted as we are from feeling, prone
to those lapses from the mutual whereby
the heart is comforted, we typify
all novel loves – lie back, replace the phone
receiver, its pre-emptive dial tone
the prelude to an unforthcoming sigh.
I think of you as much as may be thought
before minds slip, and even tempers tilt –
with privileges of private disarray –
to one degree extremer than they ought;
before fair balance goes, good milk is spilt,
and each proposed idea becomes cliché.

Rook and Crow
(from "Grave Nursery Rhymes")

Blackbird, raven, crow and rook
Drawn in margins of my book,
If I were a character
In some foreign fairy tale
It would be for you I'd look;

Stitched in old magenta pink, --
Not the finch or bobolink,
Not the jay or cardinal,
You are who I'd long for, long
With a leather vest, I think.

You would know me as Rose Red.
Down a stormy moor, misled,
Sketched in charcoal, we would go,
Blackbird, raven, rook and crow:
Friends and loves lost, maimed or dead.

Self-Portrait As Marie Laveau, Voodoo Queen of New Orleans

Don't claim this corner of my shop lacks air,
and is too dark to be appreciated –
not here, where I am happy and surrounded
with warped and webbed familiars, tokens, where
glare never comes, and nothing has a cost.
I hear a wailing, pagan call to prayer,
and wonder if, indeed, I've gotten lost;
if Christ, in all high gravity, astounded
by my pained superstitions, hasn't crossed
me off his list. A cat should have this chair,
long-whiskered, barely breathing, well-behaved,
to gracefully rebound from broken wicker
to metal threshold at the front screen door.
Don't censure it for having loved the shade,
 the *gris-gris* pouch. This corner of the store,
couched in angora cushions, *fleur-de-lis*
of iron or rope-tied fur, possesses light
enough to showcase burlap, skull and barrel.
I haven't held a thing, I haven't paid.
I'm captured by the art of what is free.
Don't call this ante-chamber too beguiled.
I'm stricken by the art in what is hard.
The fortune teller warned me as a child
never to elucidate the cards.

"Good morning, little girl," he said, and smiled,
en route between his sympathies. Well-known
to him was this desire to stand alone
among the magic trappings, dust and wax.

Beside me, in repressing reverie,
a mannequin brunette extends one hand
for potions mixed to make her beauty last.
Museums elevate our sordid facts.
She will be fixed forever, understand.
Within this twilight, everything is fair,
for everything observed is indistinct:
a court, a case, an intimated lair
for sundry shriving shadows on the toe,
brown sugar and confections, space to think.
Reflections from the other side lay bare
a slave's regrets when it is time to go.

This is the place one's palette turns to coal,
one's bed turns to a pallet, stately taste
to grime upon the palate, where the whole
vivid giddiness of feeling goes to waste,
and pride and moral posture rot.
                                    Two blocks
away, as many years ago, two painters
from Paris came to Royal Street, the *rue*
of red impressions. Exhibitions primed,
they strewed a show of poppies on thick stalks,
traced ladies – no display was ever quainter,
but this is not a jocular salon
in which the lingerie of life is drawn.

A premonition of cremated milk
enthralls my sense of smell, a walnut clock
upsets my sense of the contemporary,
its face immortalizing the fourth hour.

I disturb the fringe cord tiebacks, cayenne bowl.
There is no shame in touch for texture's sake.
The sugar pralines in a week will sour.
Seclusion is the ransom of the soul.

Should You Ask At Midnight

What would I do without your voice to wake me?
Cor ad cor loquitur, I'm loath to know.
Kitsch operas sound, unhesitant to shake me,
The sheers undrawn, the heavens hardly showing,
My camisole askew, of lace-trimmed black –
Not red, not white; not passionate or pure.
I raise the volume, and the voices crack—
Vanilla scores: accessible, obscure.
But what would I do without your certain voice?
Disjecta membra ... I am loath to think.
This negligée is sable, but my choice
If black had been forbidden, would be pink:
The blood of ballet satins, quartz, the lover,
That cut from which I never could recover.

VOGUE

Playing with princesses, coloring pages

Inked in a magazine drawn from the ages,

Muscle and modishness meet the ideal.

Marionettes in contempt of a meal

Hang – without strings – from the strength of their gazes.

Bent in your hands, their submission amazes.

Thus they become the butt ending of envy.

Leaf upon leaf, neo-classical frenzy

Saturates, contemplates, settles, bemuses –

Solving suspiciously as it confuses.

Marionette Romanova concedes

Russian orthodox custom in rosary beads.

Emeralds, peppermint-green paper forests

Accent these scenes – the lean portraits of florists.

How should one value Veruschka's expression

Shuttered in this closed photography session?

Powdered divinity candy and cushions

Cover the spreads of mid-winter editions,

Marshmallow white; for their headdress, sewn roses

Over demure or obstetrical poses.

Stunned between futures, the past and the present,

Which would you wager they find the most pleasant,

Statues descending a studio ladder?

Narrative needs little more, to forge matter.

A Succubus, You Said

A succubus you said I was, a devil,
the Gorgon or some fatal fairy child:
no mortal could you love on such a level,
not anything of earth, nor less than wild.
But never did you link me with the good.
I might have given health and hearth to be
a Muse or Grace, a laurel in your wood,
a saint or angel on your Christmas tree.
It would be pretty to pretend the heart
relies on magic, rather than alliance
with equals, but the love you laid to art
I must attribute to impartial science;
and while you saw in me all Hades, I
saw you conveying chariots through the sky.

Sylvia Plath's Chicken Crosses The Road

I will not stoop, I will not stoop
any more, old coop
in which I have layed like a slave
for thirty months, clucking and plucked,
bare between burlap and pony poop.

Farmyard, I have had to leave you,
get out while there's still time --
gunny sack grey with the bay
of prisoner puppies and porkers
round as a plump, pink squeal,

and a bay, yea, I say, a bay
at the moon, too, too, and your waters blue
for drowning the mistress's kittens: *achoo,*
Farmer Frankenstein goes as he dries out his clothes
from the kill.

I had hoped you might yield something new
with a Tatar refrain in my hen-pecking brain,
but these idiots don't have a clue,
bean-greens, green beans,
back and forth with their 18-wheel loads.
Whoo-hoo.

I used to try to appreciate you
this side of that hellish, freakish road
where I once saw a toad, feral and flattened
by a passing sedan,
a Tatar toad, I knew,
a toad from L.A., Boston, Kalamazoo.
I envied the toad.
I think I want to *be* that toad:
the old cock's in pursuit,
there's a boot in my route,
and the worm I catch early won't do.

Farmyard, you stand in my mind like a scythe,
not kindly, not blithe - a jail
with a nail in your gate,
neither rusty, trusty, nor true.
Farmyard, I have come to loathe you,

a tale in my gullet,
something stuck in my craw.
I despise categorical husbandry law,
and that fence, and this brooding, the damned weathervane, too.
Farmyard, Farmyard, you fascist. We're through.

This Night Slip, In His Honor

(after Komachi)

This night slip, in his honor
　　flipped inside out – of lace-
edged netting – is the color
　　of Shaka Zulu's face;
of panther flower at midnight
　　where crow and boa doze;
of vertigo and stage fright
　　in frail Ophelia's clothes.

I wear it as a symbol.
　　Its ripped, Chantilly trim
I fixed without a thimble,
　　was pricked and bled for him.

A torn band may be mended,
　　but what if he and I
disband, no longer blended?
　　My spine turned to the sky,
reflecting on my dresser
　　from mirror-fine sateens:
the Great Bear with the Lesser...

　　I dream of Shoji screens,
and when desire becomes
　　an overlaying itch,
the throbbing in my thumbs
　　untenable to stitch,

sleek, fitted, with the passion
  of Shaka Zulu's face,
   reversed and fringe-of-fashion,
    I put it on, in place
   of melanistic egrets,
    the vacant crystal ball.
  Victoria has secrets;
   I am her baby doll.

Till Death

For wealthy, poorer, best and better, worse,
honeymoon to formaldehyde and hearse;

in suntan and disease, forsaking all
encroachers, as it was before the Fall;

through trailer park and palace dormer, flood
and fire, through Hymen's sacrificial blood;

in fetid care and elegant abuse,
in love and out of *let us call a truce*,

at odds and even balanced, but in vain,
past Ozymandias, via wedding train;

for infidel and true believer, vows
and rites, the breath, the bone of sacred cows;

through twin and foster, stepson, only child,
from crackers in the sheets to satin-styled;

by flights from Herod to Egyptian sod
through states concluding in the birth of God

you take me, to support, unbutton, cherish,
you take me, by the pressure of this parish,

through *Sorry, Trivial Pursuit, Risk, Clue*
to cool *In Pace* from the hot *I Do*.

To the Absent Lover of the Soul

Confessions, calls – for half a week –
reserved without expression, I
was slow in coming, pained to speak,
unduly shy.

You've crises to attend, and there
are rumors You move most among
those independents who forbear
a prolix tongue.

But You should be so pleased with me,
who waited three dead sunsets through,
before I tried telepathy
to contact You.

Endeavoring to circumvent
degrees of Goat and Scorpio,
I questioned where it is You went,
and why You go.

No answer came, but that I dredged
from wishing wells of hearing – pinched
for passion, pillowed thickly, wedged
in kid and chintz.

What's there to do for rustic loves
on Tuesdays, when both earth and tile
are costly – earnestness like gloves
gone out of style –

but re-conceive one's space to make
some clear account from clouded thought,
to sail it towards You, and forsake
the overwrought?

To The Black Cat Encountering Consequence

As bad as you have been of late, by rights
You should be banished outside to the ditch,
To pay your penance in disturbing nights,
Expecting to be rescued by some witch
In morbid need of a familiar friend
With wicked eyes and automatic claws;
A mistress with few fineries to mend,
And less respect for civilizing laws.
And, child to Him who furnished flocks of quail
Until the sons of Israel were sick,
I could be glad to see you blanching pale
As milk, made prey to your own vicious tricks.
Poetic justice might keep me content –
But for those pleading eyes, when you repent.

To A Creole Lady
by Charles Baudelaire

Within a perfumed land caressed by sun,
I've known, beneath empurpled trees and palms
Where idleness into the eyes will run,
A Creole woman's unregarded charms.

Her skin is pale and warm; brunette enchantress
With throat of noble manner and allure;
Tall and svelte in motion like a huntress.
Her smile is tranquil and her eye is sure.

My lady, should you walk true glory's lands
Along the grassy Loire or the Seine's strands,
Beauty fit to deck antique estates
You'd make, in these secluded, shadowed parts,
Sprout a thousand sonnets in the poets' hearts,
Whom your grand eyes would make more servile than your slaves.

To a Lady Contemplating Mischief

Encompassed at all corners by such fine
a cadre of companions, knights and flags
as could be wished by any modern mistress
between her piles of trashy plastic bags,
take care you mind your station and your manners.

As hallowed as the doe or white-faced owl;
as basic as black-standard-bearing banners;
as crucial as the Cross and cleric's cowl
are these to you, who have no other place
of peace except in syndicate of fairies,
etched-glass affections, unpretentious grace,
waxen, lit wicks, remorse and pale *Hail Mary's.*

Ignore the crass; observe – if there is need –
cats' cradles, china, the Apostle's Creed...

To My Baudelaire

Since loving you the moment we first met,
I have consented always to be bound
In misericords preventative of sound,
In brutal rooms beneath the *oubliette*,
With rotten rag, soiled gag, mock-leather threat.

Sour bandages, they mortify around
What heart I have, here in our underground,
At rest with this arousal to regret.

I am the tied, with you, the undertaken:
Here I, your undertaker, disinfectant
Gloves behind me, digging either wrist –
A riven cinch, blindfolded wench, expectant
As ninth-month Mary with her God-forsaken
Oblation – wait securely to be kissed.

Ursulines, After the Storm

Beside St. Anthony's Garden,
behind the white cathedral,
in the Vieux Carré, where hurricanes
have ripped two priceless oaks,
is Pirate's Alley, where the turquoise doors
and salmon-lacquered frames run under roofs
embedded with the glass of broken bottles.

A bar or rough café, two missing walls –
laid-bare-to-air arrangements – opening
to south and east, broadcasts the breaking news
from CNN. The place is free of smoke,
the dim interior too weirdly calm.
       (One wonders if they'll ever speak again).

An hour from now, a woman will sit down
inside St. Louis on the hindmost pew,
to have her picture taken in the dark.
Her round face will develop cyanotic,
her sloe eyes like the eyes of tawny owls.
The latticework confessionals are latched,
empty and fat, with no one to confess.
       (One wonders if they'll ever sin again).

"Ladies, girls! Come in! Earn while you learn,"
she'd hear, if priest and pimp were to exchange
their pitches. Then the noise on Bourbon Street

would be a call to worship, Latin chant,
and pre-teen girls intent to keep themselves
for Jesus Christ, would find themselves in brothels,
prostitutes find themselves in pristine habits.
       (One wonders if they'll ever pray again).

The Vampire
By Charles Baudelaire

You who like a stabbing sword
Entered in my plaintive heart;
You who like a forceful horde
Of demons, wines, crazed and with art,
Of my humiliated soul
To make your bed and your domain
--Infamous one, to whose control
I'm bound, like convicts to the chain,
Like alcoholics to the cruet,
Like stubborn gamblers to their play,
Like scavengers to their decay,
--Accursed, accursed be you!
I have implored the rapid blade
To conquer my independence,
And told perfidious, poison aide
To help my confidence.
Alas! The poison and the sword
Disdainfully have said to me:
"You've not the worth to be restored
From your confounded slavery.
Imbecile! – from her empire,
If our travails delivered you
Your kisses only would renew
The cadaver of your vampire."

Vampires of Youth

Still, on twig stools under concert pianos,
listless, they're stammering Bach's best concertos.

Stained with repasts from some previous evening
feast, they are lingering, stiffened and yellow.

Waistbands of bandage, historical sleeving
twisted, they're hungering; yarns made to mellow.

Molded through mist, looking out on marsh mallow,
over one skin-stinging moment they sorrow –
blistered eternity turning their halos
tarnished, their hostels to stranglehold shallows.

Variations on a Fantasy

Your mistress died on Monday night,
after she'd sent me postcards signed
in red ink, using our last name.
She choked on chocolates. Such a shame.
Your mistress died on Tuesday morning,
after she'd sent me pictures of
herself in briefs you bought last summer.
She drowned in red Chianti. Bummer.
Your mistress died at Wednesday's door,
after our daughter's wedding shower,
where she'd shown up, red-lipped and blushed.
Her limo crashed and burned. I'm crushed.
Your mistress died today at noon,
after she'd left a message on
our old machine which wasn't clear:
bludgeoned with pearls. So sorry, dear.

Watching New Orleans Drown

"My life has been spared to mourn for you,
Not to freeze over your memory as a weeping willow..."
Anna Akhmatova
Seventh Book

Some of us could have cried, "Take us instead."
The banks of Babylon are over sown
with willows, and its exiles overfed.
None of us can insist he is alone,
but the hand of God has snapped in Jackson Square.
Dear Christ! Cathedral oaks, forever gone,
are lying with their roots exposed to air,
unlivened by the Lord they fell upon.

The Court of Two Sisters, with its lights and ferns
like jungle Christmas – has it gone to sea?
We play the violinist while Rome burns,
it seems: a corpse-in-progress elegy –
messages painted with primer on a roof,
intended to be gathered from the sky,
as grasping as the thunder was aloof,
and sober as the driest eye is dry.

The academic tongue gives way to threats.
The heart of ice can find no voice at all.
We're told domestic aid and foreign debts.
The Dome is torn. For days the levee wall

has poured. Canal Street lives up to its name.
Humanity's a marker in the flood
where black wrought iron islets are aflame
between rifle fire and Mississippi mud.

Armed National Guards and Coastmen come in hosts;
Parks statewide engorge with makeshift tents
of refugees incompetent as ghosts.
The bridge across Lake Ponchartrain's a fence
of broken chain link. Burning, burning, burning;
convention center chaos. Stench. Disaster,
while somewhere else, the world continues turning,
and Magdalen whimpers *Master, Master, Master,*

Lock down the Crown ... 1st Cavalry, Marines;
policing house to house amid reports
ten thousand souls have fled their fleshly miens.
Plumbagos drop blue blossoms in the courts.
Elysian Fields has turned to Styx; a man
is tied against a signpost. *Esplanade*'s
expectant belles scrape mandarins from a can,
hearing the shunt of helicopter blades.

A woman sobs beside her shrouded spouse.
Shattered hotel room windows wave white sheets,
surreal surrender of a regal house.
The sights initiate what sense completes,
our *coup de maître* of breath, *élan* and culture
become a riverboat vacation through
museums to the cannibal and vulture –
a silt of every art we ever knew.

The Way I See It

You come back to pack up a few last things
before you settle in D.C. for good.
The bell sounds, voices call, your cell phone rings.
If anyone would answer them, *you* would.
Instead, you find me waiting, lonely there,
between the stair and foyer, I would bet,
and sliding fingers through your thick black hair,
you neither turn, neglect me, nor forget,
but with the calm precaution of a prince
witnessing kin and kingdom go to sea,
you tell me of the melancholy, wince,
and say you've found brief confidence in me,
putting me, for one brilliant trice, above
insistence, time, and everything you love.

What Shall You Say?

By Charles Baudelaire

What shall you say this evening, solitary soul?
What shall you say, my heart, heart withered heretofore,
To the very good, the very dear, the beautiful
Whose divine regard has brought you into bloom once
more?

--To sing her praise, we set aside our haughtiness.
Nothing is equal to her sweet authority;
The perfume of angels, her spiritual flesh,
And her eye clothes us again in clothes of clarity.

Regardless if it be by night, in solitude,
Regardless if in the street and in the multitude,
Her phantom dances like a torch within the air.

At times, it speaks: "I'm fair, and I command," we hear it
Say, "For love of me, love nothing but the Fair.
I am your Muse, Madonna, and your guardian Spirit."

Widow

She rested in the crevice of a socket
internal in the shed's devolving brick,
set high: jet-figured, lacquer-legged and thick,
smooth, huge, coiled up with cunning in a pocket
of cartilage web, to match the bone-white moths
ensnarled in her embroidery.

                                        A stick
of fig or oak I used some days to prick
her into action, not for torment, but
for fond experiment. That she could glut
herself on blood and sickened flight, yet keep
my wonder and affection never seemed
to trouble me, nor that a dainty slut
could hold me as her method-eaten loves.

Oh, she: so hour-glassed and so detached
from scruple, in desire so badly matched...

Most days, the shed was stifling, moist, the air
dolorous with the pine of mourning doves,
yet comforting, with us together there,
elite as polish, intricate as sin,
in tar and darkness, oil and mildew stain,
without a sound, digesting charm within;
and, sweating from the breadth of every pore,
who will have died when I want nothing more,
I might have suffocated to remain.

With Red Ink from the Vieux Carré

I miss the wake of spearmint and tobacco
pursuing you along these alleyways
I've clung to like an orphan since my youth.
The Square in seasoned autumn bears an echo
of Jackson's coldness, and the pink displays
azaleas make inside wrought iron courts
would please you, with the smell of sweet vermouth
and innocence, and fall ash, and bravado.
Du Monde still brews your loathed *café au laits*,
but love's no cheaper on Saint Ann, in truth,
than when, by Creole gentlemen's reports,
Marie LaVeau submitted it for sale.
The Mississippi, weeping past her ports,
still cringes when confronted with a wale.

The Xanthippic Scholar From Seton

There once was a writer from Seton
who labeled his lover a cretin;
"The proof of your notion,
my dear? My devotion,"
retorted the lady, unbeaten.

You would take to bed the cosmos...
By Charles Baudelaire

You would take to bed the cosmos as a whole,

Impure *femme.* Boredom renders cruel your soul.

To exercise your teeth at this one game,

You have to rack a new heart every day.

Your eyes, illuminated like boutiques,

Or like flamboyant lamps at public feasts,

Insolently using borrowed potency

Without acquaintance with the law of beauty.

Blind, deaf machine, fecund in the cruel!

Drinker of the world's blood, useful tool,

How can you have no shame, before all mirrors

Not estimating your allurements paler?

Never recoiling, at this evil's size,

Behind with fear, where you believe you're wise,

When Nature, great within its masked intents

Employs itself, o woman, queen of sins,

--From you, vile beast, -- a genius to have rolled?

O grand ignominy! Sublime of mold!

Zydeco Daybreak
(Morning on the Mississippi Delta)

The courtyard pigeons' claws
pad past across mossed brick,
their mottled bodies thick
with mystic fruit. They pause
and stare at us, as though
awaiting from our hands
caresses, or the strands
of sweet banana dough.

With pride – or something like –
beside the wrens they strut,
now fast, now slow, then jut
their chests at nothing, strike
at palms with ruby beaks.

Sub-tropic sunlight streaks
the patio, clay urns
and terra cotta pots
made warm as shadow dots
the Resurrection Ferns.

The air no longer heavy,
our French cathedral chimes
with faith and hope ten times
its notes across the levee.

Ghost and Guest

Collapsing on a sleeping friend
Upon the couch, I fell
Sincerely sorry to offend
This guest in my "hotel."

Our customary schedules changed,
He lay as if in pitch,
No boundaries, his form estranged
From which idea was which.

He panted thrice, but barely stirred,
His fright dry and compressed –
Neither of us with a word,
We two: the ghost and guest.

My pulse stopped years ago, it's true.
That person is a ghost
Who stumbles; this, perhaps, he knew –
Unseeing, yet engrossed.

I fled the scene in full control,
Apologies *ad hoc.*
My terrorizing of a soul
Had come as little shock.

Sonnets from the Dark Lady

Russia's poet, the great Anna Akhmatova, posed the question: "Could Beatrice have conceived like Dante? Or Petrarch's Laura glorified the heat of love?" Indeed, through the immortal achievement of Christina Rossetti's sonnet sequence, the *Monna Innominata,* we have seen what might have been the answer in poetry. And now – who remains to answer their lords, among the great loves of literature? What if the Dark Lady of William Shakespeare's sonnets should step forth from the shadows, to show *her* fashions?

1.

"In the old age black was not counted fair,..."

The world knows black as universal sin.
No Paris stylist passionately swearing
The *chic* are rendered more chic, thin more thin,
Persuades the *bon vivant* into its wearing.
In black, the child is chased away, affection
And understanding, though it clothe demurely;
Compassion, color run from the complexion.
But since life thrives through compromises, surely
Let raven, sable, rook be my disguise.
Make murk my brow, in ashes root my hair,
That while I live, none but my master's eyes
May gain one aureole to find me fair,
And thereby – in fair finding – obfuscate
My mirror's counter and uncountered mate.

2.

"...I envy those jacks that nimble leap,
to kiss the tender inward of thy hand..."

What do I envy, love, that touches thee?
Too much. More to the point I'd prove to list
Things un-provocative of jealousy,
But label me a cureless columnist.
Domestic sodas and imported beers
Upon thy lips I envy, dark or light;
Slow musicals whose tongues sink in thine ears
Burgundy preludes; nightmares which at night
Awaken thee, and through the day remain
Reminders of your haunting in the sheets.
I envy seats beside thee, filled in vain
Amid an auditorium of seats;
Thy sport coat's tweed *mélange* of silhouette
And loosened negligence of etiquette.

3.

"The expense of spirit in a waste of shame
Is lust in action…"

Say Love is useless, shameful, overwrought
In shape and bent. Call Love the expertise
Of idiots, a flagellant of thought
Making a victim of itself to please;
Unprofitable, disrespected, trampled,
A rose bench in a peach conservatory
Where sugar canes *ad nauseam* are sampled –
A subjugated shade of lust's red glory;
Call Love a forger's counterfeit of peace,
Naïve, complacent, loose, unkempt, forthcoming,
Archaic, quaint, a traitor true, a grease.
Regardless, women will continue humming
As if it meant dementia to despise
This Neat Suite sham, this No-Man's Paradise.

4.

"My mistress' eyes are nothing like the sun…"

Milord makes rare parade of his emotions.

Completing undertakings at the pew,

No braggart sagas follow his devotions;

His myths are masked, reported visions few.

Inviting me to drink but not to dance,

He sheds no tears departing from my bed.

He has one sole, uninterrupted glance.

I have for faith the sacrificed unsaid.

Many a diva gets her burning word,

Chocolate oblations brandied, blessed, hot-toddied.

I have for heat the hidden and unheard,

An incandescent, backwards disembodied,

And would – for naught and nothing – make a trade

For pageants staged within him, well-displayed.

5.

"A thousand groans but thinking on thy face..."

Deliciously, in last night's dream, in stark
Chromatic semitones of silver gloom,
A gangly actress groping through blind dark,
I found you, as I tapped around the room –
Lounged out along a couch in moonlight, still
And waiting for me in the shriveled mist
Of atmosphere, beneath a windowsill.
I knelt, my fist against you, and we kissed.
Then, rousing to remember and write down
The gist for you, I felt a stabbing pain
Behind the ribs and bodice of my gown,
Where hands had been too heavy to remain.
The finale our *opus* to be finished,
What's meant by *minor, seventh* and *diminished?*

6.

"Then will I swear beauty herself is black..."

From adolescence favoring the blanch
Of white in mood and dress, the ingénue
Eventually sees one cannot stanch
The blood that stains – and so one turns to blue.
But blue, requiring peace at all expense
For maintenance of character, will bleed
Away shade's prejudice, whence preference
Must soon emerge for black – black which indeed
Will line the eyes like little else, to mourn.
Kohl paint creates no statement in the city,
Making it doubtful one was ever born,
And therefore better fit for eyeing pity.
Accuse, laugh, weep, or – dumb – avert thy face.
Black's hale enough to hold the frail, with grace.

7.

"But slave to slavery my sweet'st friend must be?"

No erudite professor speaking Persian,
No boy Bohemian, no bantam dancer,
No market magnate dangling an excursion
Before me through the Tropic band of Cancer
By silver ports, no squire in English suede
Mounting to hounds about his privileged lawn,
No lank composer with some strange *aubade*
Commencing whence I turn to him at dawn,
No friend of thine, no friend of mine, no Rhodes
Scholar, nor Colossus of the same,
No mathematician bearing lyric codes
To solve my single status, bears a name
Or face but thine – nor else to the above –
I come by, call or covet, making love.

8.

"The statute of thy beauty thou wilt take…"

My eyes were beggar's red, not black, for days
Beyond those laggard moments when I saw
You leaning towards her with a wide-eyed gaze,
Compounded callowly with schoolboy awe –
So casual. My lids wore nothing bold
As black, but screened themselves in suits of nudes
Which changed them haggard, tedious, too old…
Who profits through peroxide attitudes?
Designers advocate faint apricot
In blusher, for more catholic appeal.
I'm drawn between the neutral, chill and hot –
Her visage pure, impassioned, round and real.
Perhaps a dash of ruby would become
This tired reflection. Or profounder plum.

9.

"Whoever hath her wish, thou hast thy will…"

Like a jeweler recognizing ruby, look
Down at this mouth, observe the staining gloss
Its Cupid's Bow and pouting corners took
Between the ashen sand of cheek and cross.
Christen me *Ruby,* thinking of the dunes,
Sand-powdered sphinx with delta underneath
And make a mummery of my dry runes,
As though I spoke with gemstones in my teeth.
Or Ruby, for the rubbing of a bottle –
The domicile I must desert through smoke,
Devising thee thy wishes, but to mottle
Their consummation with some genii joke,
Then, against my flagon's cabochon, encrust
Our *mutual* fantasy, as you, too, must.

10.

"Swear to thy blind soul that I was thy Will..."

Existent in the *will* of comprehension,
Upheld by both the foresight and the hind,
Are bounds and bonds about which future tension,
Admitting love with distance, holds in mind.
If I *will* hold thee, I will hold thee, seeing
Or blind, or – best – peripherally skilled:
That most appropriate outlook of being
For one en-bonded to the richer-willed.
Come nearer, clearer conscience loses sight.
Remain away, and vision cannot see,
Yet to see and hold too closely will invite
A will of window-wishing not to be.
Withhold, bequeath, cry *bankrupt*, owe or bill;
You hold that ruby title which is will.

11.

"In things right true, my heart and eyes have erred..."

Because my viewer is denied the vision
Some label evil, others quality,
A vintage crop of silences, derision,
Or judgment passing for frivolity
veneers our covert confidence. I rank
That voice and conversation the crescendo
Of all – its depths fermented Muscat, dank
Or Asti sweet, profaning innuendo
In its superior ranges. Intuition
However would appear to him nonsense,
Thus, I manifest as vineyard apparition –
Discourse without desire for recompense;
Because he tastes few favored among wine,
And even less for savoring of mine.

12.

"Thus, vainly thinking that she thinks I'm young..."

My love, lured by the mirror, stands erect,
Adjusts his collar band, cufflink and tie,
Assessing fit and finish, to reflect
On what will break before it speaks a lie:
This looking glass which will, when I undress,
Have been a witness to the unforeseen.
Some seeing us in love together guess
My love to be the elder, I the green
And younger – his *gamine*, his preening lass;
Though greater years have weighted me with curses,
And as attested by this looking glass
Vouching for truth, even while it reverses,
So vision would be blindness to surmise
I am not veteran, lying winter-wise.

13.

"Wound me not with thine eyes, but with thy tongue…"

You're written off: *Stage Up, pursued by Sloth,*
A burlap blindfold tied in Gordian knot
Around thy temples, soddening the cloth,
Flex-glue left from some farce of *Camelot.*
Eyes veiled, thou could'st of course do with a *saw.*
I reach into my sleeve of coven black,
Withdrawing by one ruby-polished claw
Its proper Christian designation: *Hack.*
No slack with which thou might'st manipulate
The intricacies of this hitch, unravel
Its whorls, nor broadsword like that Greek, the Great,
I script for thee infernal, restless travel,
Blinded as flying vermin, vacant rooks,
And Woman's ever-batting, vapid looks.

14.

"Be wise as thou art cruel..."

Hex the stitches, hex the stockings, hex
The notches, brooches, sash and zipper screw
Of every form among my fairer sex
Who ever shared a sleepless night with you.
On every button bitten in nocturnal
Remissions of immaculacy, chaste
Observance of composure, let eternal
Corrosion live with acid aftertaste.
Her laces be corrupted with a bruise
Like excrement – no soothing mauves or violets.
May vomit varnish her Messina shoes,
And bullock filth her easy, urban eyelets.
Those grave clothes guttering, let drip with drool
Each night's remembrance of each rutted ghoul.

15.

"In faith, I do not love thee…"

Considering thy flighty dearth of care
Remains, at worst, an ordinary pain –
The swamp's mosquito, pessimist of air,
Perpetuated through a stagnant rain –
I wonder if you've found me in this mud
Beneath the cypress, meaning to take my breath
Away, and for a moment sip my blood,
Or merely nip until I've bled to death.
In me, a thousand blemishes are noted,
Not least of them, a kinship with that pest
Whose bayou bitterness afflicts both boated
And shored, in any vessel caught at rest.
But verily, while a pathogenic vector,
I would – like thee – I could advance on nectar.

16.

"Those lips of thine that have profaned their scarlet ornament..."

My lips aren't ornamented in bright scarlet
Or crimson lipsticks, luminous of shade
And drama, for the harlequin, the harlot,
The hallmark. *Dateless Ruby* is the name
For this specific recipe of red.
If it be true their color has appealed
To untrue love, to burglarize some bed
And to false lovers make their pledges – sealed
Or loosened – I at least would have them known
For what they truly are: a-spread with jewel,
Without a date, so as it were alone,
And at their darkest, crowning – if not cruel –
With lasting stain elaboration, though
You smear, in clear-cut, ruby Cupid's Bow.

17.

"Lo, as a careful housewife runs to catch..."

Here are no stone Madonnas on my rugs,
Enshrouding the Child by various embraces
With varied faces, in shawls or shrugs
On Galilee silks or high piano cases.
Within their smiles is found too little art
For representing porous mystery,
And whether metaphoric myths impart
Direction to one's run, or history,
The *really* careful soul will realize
Like Bethany's lax sister, that to chase
A flying feather while the loved one cries
Is poor art on a rich Madonna's face,
And catching it is no authentic catch.
Love, I am not thy mother, but thy match.

18.

"Two loves I have, of comfort and despair..."

Around the little bottle called Desire
I let my conscience and caresses linger.
No warning date inscribed there, whence expire
Its side-effects, on ring and middle finger
I balance it in study, run a thumb
Around its rim, until I'm ill, until
Its contents spill, until its contents come
To puddles on the floor, of pang and pill.
Despair would chew them well, as overdose,
Comfort would gulp them – an holistic cure –
Even though now eerie with the gross
Pollution from the ground: disbursed, impure,
Each chanting like a spinstered, nursing shrew,
"Desire, this bottled hell, I hate – not you."

19.

"and saved my life, saying 'not you'…"

Eight days through Egypt in the eye
Of Ra were not enough to bake
This saturation in me dry
Of heat, although I were to take
The "not" from "Him I do despise…"
My "not" remains, for I would *knot*
His wrists and ankles with the ties
Of feeling nevermore forgot,
Nor weakened through the slaving sun
Of Cairo. If it kept him warm,
Though, I might let my loops undone
And lay a liberating storm
On him at dusk, when sun grows vague,
To whet him – like the Seventh Plague.

20.

"So shalt thou feed on Death, that feeds on men."

Thou, Worm, whose hunger in my mother's grave
Now gnaws at her with inartistic duty,
Have made my heart an artificial slave
To horror: chewer of breath-empty beauty.
Night-crawler, beetle, spider, termite, louse –
Could I retain contempt for any creature
Desiring such a rosy, homeless house?
Is hatred at thy feast our common feature?
Decay as passion, dung and monument,
Our necessary pact – with the conceit
In eking ecstasy from discontent –
I finish with my flourished signature,
Gay grief at garnishing Death's garniture.

21.

"My love is as a fever, longing still..."

When still a silly girl, I dreamed there came
From far away, with fame, a star who fell
At my front walkway: wounded, weak, and lame,
Whom I alone had power to make well.
Abed for days with fever, damp and prone
To alternate from numbness into flush,
He languished as I listened to him moan,
Leaning above him, cautious not to brush
Against his fits. What Heaven had decreed
Was that I heal, not aggravate, nor nurse
Tenacious aftertastes of my own need,
Forbidding me. And so, now reimburse,
Endure not cure, but care; now, if thou will,
Below me moan, Belovèd. Lie, long still.

22.

"O cunning Love! with tears thou keep'st me blind..."

I wish my rooms were hung with London vapor.
I wish my walls were spiral-staired, and scrolled.
I wish your words were more than drape and paper.
I wish you were the scared one, I the scold.
I wish that Samhain weren't my hour of birth.
I wish it were a bright gem set in June.
I wish I kept thee not with tears but mirth.
I wish I weren't your pale, pathetic moon.
I wish that I could be the sun to you.
I wish you could see verity in tears.
I wish my ruby slippers were true blue.
I wish they hadn't faded through the years.
I wish you'd let the slandered Hero die.
I wish you loved me when you didn't cry.

23.

"Can'st thou, O cruel, say I love thee not?"

If I were both thy mistress and thy muse,
From all conceivable reactions, chief
Among my choices – if I had to choose –
Would be the innocence of disbelief.
You see all by aurora, analyze
All brilliant day displays, and so aware
Am I of these foul faults, that from such eyes
I would hide in oblivion, lest they compare
Me sickly with the witches from thy past.
Hence I will hold thee in the dark, denied
The disappointments of a love held fast.
If darkness blinds, in truth, it never lied,
And while he praise the perfect, pure, and good,
Man cannot love what is not understood.

24.

"The more I hear and see just cause of hate..."

The more I hear and see just cause of hate
Within this wanting world, the more I see
Just cause to warranty at bargain rate
My comprehension, credit, sympathy.
I cannot be all things to all, but this
I take into consideration when
Perfection would betray me with a kiss
And leave me with a heretic *Amen*.
That if I condescend to that which wants –
Deficiency and Want themselves are truth,
And self-conceit a paltry vice to daunt
For a word which in our language rhymes with "youth."
Time is a tick's infection whence we die.
We may as well be humble, you and I.

25.

"Then, gentle cheater, urge not my amiss…"

The will I love, that voice and stamina
I will not tangle with too much temptation.
Thou art my words, my wit, my *anima*.
They'll die with thee a paper moon's cremation.
Rise at my reputation like Apollo,
My joy. In my eclipses sink, fall deep
Asleep. Like Hestia, I will smile and swallow
vernacular desire, to stay and keep
Awake the hearth of conscience with thy flame,
Thy rise acute as sunrise to arouse.
And as demurring Hestia became
The mistress of her holy lover's house,
Forsaking pride to handle his affairs,
So will I stoke thy prize, clasped unawares.

26.

"For all my vows are oaths but to misuse thee…"

Misuse makes for its costume gorgeous ghosts
Of garments any critic could revere.
O how I hate them fresh – the grandiose
And homeliest alike, opaque or sheer,
Both rose and jet. Just those reduced to wraiths
Hold true appeal. In those I put my wear,
And then the *Holy* Ghost – well in my Faith's
Constraints, no matter what you see or swear.
Thus when you vow by me, you vow by rag
Dampened with swamp wine, with a Host of earth
Rubbed through its threads, embellished with moss slag.
To vow by me is to avow a birth
Conception so neglected as to make
My own kin call its summons a mistake.

27.

"I, sick withal, the help of bath desired..."

Scheherazade, reclining on a bolster
Of sand-washed, woven satins, kept awake
Her shah with yarns befitting to upholster
A pallet of the most discerning *sheik.*
The legends hint extenuated life
And glory she, by moonlight, sought –the tomb
More dire than the allegiance of a wife
To sick, disheartened rule. Don't let's presume.
To linger with her lord's commanding diction
She could have bathed him in her tales – each tassle
Tinged with strange or scientific fiction –
One thousand and one *more* witching hours, gracile
And moving as a lunar phase among
The solar pulses of her master's tongue.

Acknowledgments

"because the cut your presence," "Prima Donna," "Lining Up for the Tower of Terror," "The Murderess," "Evening Harmony" by Charles Baudelaire first appeared in *Able Muse*. "In Days to Come" first appeared in *American Arts Quarterly*. "By This Pitch & Motion," "Ursulines, After the Storm" first appeared in *The Avatar Review*. "Sylvia Plath's Chicken Crosses the Road" first appeared in *Bumbershoot*. "The Eye Passes," "Mark My Words" first appeared in the revived *Botteghe Oscure* (Online). "Sonnets from the Dark Lady" #4, 5, 21, 23 first appeared in *The Chimaera*. "Line to Circle," On the Anniversary of a Natural Disaster," "Sonnets from the Dark Lady," #10, 11 first appeared in *Chronicles: A Magazine of American Culture*. "Halloween Queen of Hearts," "Instructions for the Cemetery Cake" first appeared in *Danse Macabre*. "This Night Slip, In His Honor" first appeared in *The Dark Horse*. "Sonnets from the Dark Lady," #27, "The Lady Who Lives Here" appeared first in *The Flea*. "To a Lady Contemplating Mischief," "To the Black Cat Encountering Consequence," "Despair" first appeared in *First Things*. "French Quarter Singer," "Gentle Country," "Lady Grey," "Civic Centre," "To a Creole Lady, by Charles Baudelaire" first appeared in *Iambs & Trochees*. "Rook and Crow" first appeared in *Light Quarterly*. "The Vampire," "You would take to bed the cosmos…" by Charles Baudelaire first appeared *in Lucid Rhythms*. "The Night Without" first appeared in *The Lyric*. "Watching New Orleans Drown," "Variations on a Fantasy," "If we're to make this work…" "Sonnets from the Dark Lady," 14, 15 first appeared in *MEASURE*. "Widow," "Sunday Morning on Jackson Square," "Blind Concessions," "Litany" & "Sonnets from the Dark Lady," poems 1-3 & 16-19 first appeared in *Mezzo Cammin*. "For the Haunted Child," "Proposal," "The Way I See It", "The Final Toast," "What Shall You Say," by Charles Baudelaire, "Sonnets from the Dark Lady" 24, 26, "Considering Dolphins," "Deepwater Horizon Oil Spill in the Gulf of Mexico," "VOGUE," "In These Photographs, My Rival…" "What's Really Wrong," "Ghost & Guest" first appeared in *The National Review*. "Noli Me Tangere," "Self-Portrait as Marie Laveau," "Vampires of Youth" first appeared in *The Nepotist*. "Blue-Crested Cry" first appeared in *POETRY*. "Mardi Gras Mannequin," "The Charm of Candelabras," "Millenium Park,"

"A Succubus, You Said," "Till Death," "Corner Memorials," Dark Lady #22 first appeared in *The Raintown Review*. "In the House of Disguises," "Her Feet," "To My Baudelaire" first appeared in *SCR*. "As Van Gogh Must Have Seen," "Harlequins By Hurricane Lamp," first appeared in *THINK Journal*. "Sonnets from the Dark Lady" 5, 7, 9, "Minor Sonnet," "At the Crypt of Marie Laveau," "Zydeco Daybreak" first appeared in *TRINACRIA*. "With Red Ink from the Vieux Carré" first appeared in *Tucumcari Literary Review*. "How I Want You," "Fire Mount," first appeared in *Umbrella*. "As Always," "Should You Ask at Midnight," "Formula," "Sonnets from the Dark Lady, "poem 13 first appeared in *Unsplendid*.

Jennifer Reeser has published two previous collections of poetry (including *An Alabaster Flask*, winner of the Word Press First Book Prize, 2003, which X. J. Kennedy, poet and former editor of *The Paris Review*, wrote "...ought to have been a candidate for a Pulitzer.") Her honors include The New England Prize, The Lyric Memorial Prize, and awards from Dr. Alfred Dorn of The World Order of Narrative and Formalist Poets. Her writing has been featured on the World Wide Web editions of *POETRY* , *Verse Daily*, *Goodreads* and *E-verse Radio*, and has appeared in numerous anthologies, including Longman's college text, *An Introduction to Poetry*, edited by Dana Gioia and X. J. Kennedy. She has contributed poems, scholarly articles and translations of French and Russian literature to publications including *POETRY*, *The Hudson Review*, *Light Quarterly*, *The Formalist*, *Mezzo Cammin*, the Rockford Institute's *Chronicles: A Magazine of American Culture*, *First Things*, and *The National Review*. She works as a consultant on the faculty of the West Chester Poetry Conference, the nation's largest annual conference on poetry. She is the former assistant editor to *Iambs & Trochees*, and lives amid the bayous of southern Louisiana with her husband and children.

12494484R00079

Made in the USA
Charleston, SC
09 May 2012